Explore Space!

Exploring Mars

by Deborah A. Shearer

Consultant:
James Gerard
Aerospace Education Specialist
NASA Aerospace Education Services Program

Bridgestone Books
an imprint of Capstone Press
Mankato, Minnesota

Bridgestone Books are published by Capstone Press
151 Good Counsel Drive, P.O. Box 669, Mankato, Minnesota 56002
http://www.capstone-press.com

Library of Congress Cataloging-in-Publication Data
Shearer, Deborah A.
    Exploring Mars / by Deborah A. Shearer.
    p. cm.—(Explore space!)
    Includes bibliographical references and index.
    Contents: Exploring Mars—Early missions to Mars—First Mars landing—Mars pathfinder—Mars meteorites—What is Mars like?—Traveling to Mars—Living on Mars—Future missions—Hands on: Mars meteorites—Words to know—Read more—Internet sites.
    ISBN 0-7368-1399-3 (hardcover)
    1. Mars (Planet)—Exploration—Juvenile literature. [1. Mars (Planet)—Exploration. 2. Mars probes.] I. Title. II. Series.
QB641 .S482 2003
919.9′23′0421—dc21   2001008597

Summary: Introduces the past missions to Mars, describes the characteristics of Mars's environment, and explains how scientists might explore Mars in the future.

Editorial Credits
Christopher Harbo, editor; Karen Risch, product planning editor; Steve Christensen, series designer; Patrick D. Dentinger, book designer; Kelly Garvin, photo researcher

Photo Credits
NASA, cover, 4, 6, 8, 10–11, 12, 14, 16, 18
NASA Haughton-Mars Project/P. Lee, 20

1 2 3 4 5 6 07 06 05 04 03 02

Table of Contents

Mars

Exploring Mars

Mars is Earth's neighbor. But no astronaut has ever visited Mars. For many years, people could study Mars only through telescopes. Scientists want to learn more about this planet. They are looking for signs of life on Mars.

telescope
a tool that uses lenses to make distant objects seem larger and closer

5

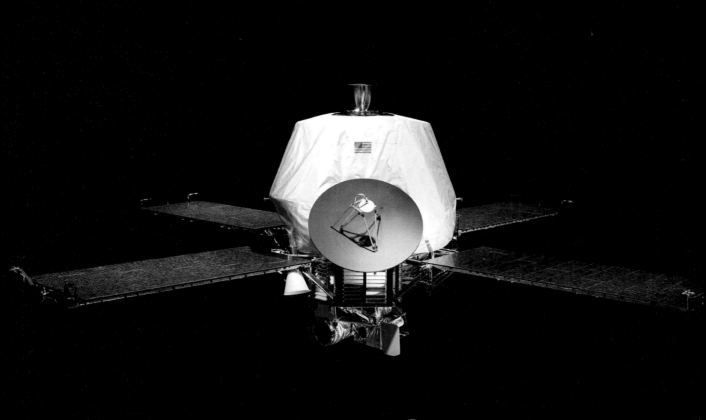

Mariner 9 took pictures of Olympus
Mons on Mars. It is the tallest volcano
in the solar system. Olympus Mons is
about three times taller than Mount
Everest, the tallest mountain on Earth.

Early Missions to Mars

Scientists have been exploring Mars since the 1960s. The United States sent Mariner 4 to Mars in 1965. This spacecraft took pictures of the surface of Mars. The United States sent another spacecraft in 1975. Mariner 9 took pictures of huge volcanoes.

surface
the top layer of something

Viking Lander
Model

8

First Mars Landing

Viking 1 and 2 were sent to Mars in 1976. Scientists used them to look for signs of life. Each spacecraft had two parts. One part orbited the planet and took pictures. The other part landed on Mars. It studied the soil and the air.

orbit
to travel around
a planet or the Sun

Pathfinder

Sojourner

Mars Pathfinder

In 1997, the Mars Pathfinder spacecraft landed on Mars. Pathfinder measured wind speeds and temperatures on Mars. It also carried a small rover called Sojourner. This remote-controlled robot moved along Mars's surface to study rocks and soil.

Scientists found a Mars meteorite in Antarctica in 1984. They believe it may have proof of past life on Mars.

Mars Meteorites

Meteorites are rocks from space that have fallen to Earth. Scientists believe some meteorites were once pieces of Mars. They have found 19 Mars meteorites on Earth. Scientists study these meteorites for signs of water and life on Mars.

Mars is called the Red Planet. Rusty iron in Mars's soil makes the planet look orange and red.

What Is Mars Like?

Mars is a rocky planet about half the size of Earth. It has several large volcanoes and deep canyons. The atmosphere on Mars is mainly carbon dioxide. An astronaut would have to wear a space suit to breathe on Mars.

carbon dioxide
a colorless, odorless gas made of carbon and oxygen

15

This NASA painting shows the type of spacecraft astronauts might use to travel to Mars.

Traveling to Mars

The distance from Earth to Mars changes. The average distance from Earth to Mars is 48 million miles (77 million kilometers). Astronauts would need six months to travel to Mars. They would need food, water, oxygen, and fuel to last at least one year.

oxygen
a colorless gas that people need to breath

This NASA painting shows machines astronauts might use to live on Mars.

Living on Mars

Astronauts would need a safe place to live on Mars. Mars can be colder than any place on Earth. Astronauts might set up a greenhouse for growing plants. They also would need machines for making oxygen and water.

Scientists test future Mars space suits in rocky deserts on Earth. This space suit was tested by the NASA Haughton-Mars Project on Devon Island in the Canadian Arctic Islands.

20

Future Missions

Many scientists hope astronauts will visit Mars in the future. Scientists are working and training to meet this goal. They are testing new fuel and studying ways to live on Mars. They are building better space suits.

Hands On: Mars Meteorites

Meteorites hit the surface of Mars and throw pieces of rock into space. These pieces of rock sometimes reach Earth. You can see how meteorites from Mars are blasted into space.

What You Need

Aluminum pie pan
Flour
Powdered chocolate milk mix
Black construction paper
Marble

What You Do

1. Fill an aluminum pie pan with flour.
2. Cover the flour by sprinkling powdered chocolate milk mix on top. The chocolate is the surface of Mars.
3. Put the black construction paper on the ground. Place the pie pan in the middle of the paper.
4. Hold the marble over the pie pan at about chest high. Drop the marble into the pie pan.

Think of the pie pan as Mars and the black paper as space. The marble is a large meteorite. Pieces of Mars fly into space when the meteorite hits. These pieces travel in space until they hit a planet like Earth. Meteorites from Mars reach Earth this way.

Words to Know

atmosphere (AT-muhss-fihr)—the mixture of gases that surrounds some planets

average (AV-uh-rij)—the most common amount of something; an average is found by adding figures together and dividing by the number of figures.

meteorite (MEE-tee-ur-rite)—a piece of rock or metal that falls from space and lands on Earth

mission (MISH-uhn)—a planned job or task

orbit (OR-bit)—to travel around a planet or the Sun

robot (ROH-bot)—a machine people program to do jobs

Read More

Kerrod, Robin. *Mars.* Planet Library. Minneapolis: Lerner, 2000.

Kipp, Steven L. *Mars.* The Galaxy. Mankato, Minn.: Bridgestone Books, 1998.

Internet Sites

Mars
http://www.windows.ucar.edu/tour/link=/mars/mars.html&edu=elem
Mars Exploration
http://mars.jpl.nasa.gov

Index